"Suffer the little children to come unto me, and forbid them not, for of such is the Kingdom of God."

-Mark 10:14

BIBLE STORIES

FOR CHILDREN

Mediatrix Press
MMXVII

ISBN: 978-1-953746-14-6

𝔍𝔪𝔭𝔯𝔦𝔪𝔞𝔱𝔲𝔯
✠ John Cardinal McCloskey

Archbishop of New York,
1892

Originally, *Bible Stories for Little Children*
Benziger Brothers, 1892

New Large Print edition:
© Mediatrix Press, 2017

Mediatrix Press
607 E. 6th Ave
Ste. 230
Post Falls, ID 8854

All Rights Reserved. This work may not be reproduced in electronic or physical format, nor placed on any website to be downloaded without the express permission of the publisher.

Table of Contents

PART I
    THE HISTORY OF THE OLD TESTAMENT

1. THE CREATION OF THE WORLD. 1

2. THE GARDEN OF PARADISE. 2

3. THE FIRST SIN. 3

4. CAIN AND ABEL. 4

5. THE DELUGE. 5

6. THE TOWER OF BABEL. 6

7. THE CALL OF ABRAHAM. 7

8. JOSEPH. 8

9. THE FAMINE. 9

10. THE CUP IN BENJAMIN'S SACK. 10

11. JOSEPH MAKES HIMSELF KNOWN TO HIS BROTHERS. . 10

12. MOSES IS BORN. 11

13. Moses' Flight. 12

14. THE BURNING BUSH. 13

15. THE PLAGUES OF EGYPT. 13

16. THE PASSAGE OF THE RED SEA. 16

17. THE QUAILS, THE MANNA, AND THE WATER IN THE DESERT..................................... 16

18. THE TEN COMMANDMENTS. 17

19. THE GOLDEN CALF............................ 19

20. THE TWELVE SPIES........................... 20

21. THE SIN OF MOSES........................... 21

22. THE BRAZEN SERPENT......................... 21

23. The Death of Moses......................... 22

24. THE ISRAELITES ENTER THE PROMISED LAND...... 22

25. THE INGRATITUDE OF THE ISRAELITES........... 23

26. SAMUEL..................................... 23

27. DAVID...................................... 25

28. DAVID AND GOLIATH.......................... 25

29. SOLOMON.................................... 27

30. THE DIVISION OF THE KINGDOM................ 28

PART II
    THE HISTORY OF THE NEW TESTAMENT

1. ELIZABETH AND MARY........................... 30

2. ZACHARY IS PUNISHED.......................... 30

3. THE ANNUNCIATION............................. 31

4. Mary Visits Elizabeth........................... 32

5. John is Born.................................... 33

6. The Birth of Jesus.............................. 34

7. The Three Wise Men.............................. 36

8. The Prophecy of Simeon.......................... 38

9. The Flight into Egypt........................... 40

10. The Feast of the Passover...................... 41

11. The Baptism of Jesus........................... 43

12. The Marriage Feast............................. 44

13. The Draught of Fishes.......................... 46

14. The Sermon on the Mount........................ 48

15. The Man Cured of the Palsy..................... 48

16. The Pool of Bethsaida.......................... 50

17. The Storm at Sea in Galilee.................... 51

18. The Daughter of Jairus......................... 52

19. The Loaves and Fishes.......................... 54

20. Jesus Walks on the Sea......................... 55

21. The Transfiguration............................ 56

22. Jesus the Children's Friend.................... 57

23. THE BLIND MAN... 58

24. THE GOOD SAMARITAN... 59

25. WE MUST FORGIVE TO BE FORGIVEN... 61

26. THE LOST SHEEP... 62

27. THE PRODIGAL SON... 64

28. THE RICH MAN AND LAZARUS... 66

29. CHRIST RAISES LAZARUS TO LIFE... 68

30. JESUS RIDES INTO JERUSALEM... 71

31. THE WIDOW'S MITE... 72

32. THE PASCHAL LAMB... 72

33. THE WASHING OF THE FEET... 73

34. THE BLESSED SACRAMENT... 75

THE PASSION OF JESUS

35. THE BETRAYAL OF JUDAS, AND PETER'S DENIAL... 77

36. JESUS IN THE GARDEN... 77

37. JUDAS BETRAYS JESUS... 79

38. JESUS BEFORE THE HIGH PRIEST... 80

39. PETER DENIES JESUS... 80

40. CAIPHAS... 81

41. Pilate. 81

42. The Scourging. 82

43. The Crowning of Thorns. 83

44. Pilate and the Jews. 84

45. The Way of the Cross. 85

46. Jesus is Nailed to the Cross. 86

47. On the Cross. 87

48. The Thieves. 88

49. Jesus Speaks to Mary. 88

50. Jesus Dies. 89

51. Jesus is Put in the Tomb. 89

52. The Resurrection. 90

53. Jesus Appears to Mary Magdalen. 91

54. Jesus Appears to His Apostles. 92

55. Peter. 93

56. The Promise of the Holy Ghost. 94

57. The Ascension. 95

The Feasts and Fasts of the Year. 97

BIBLE STORIES
for
CHILDREN

PART I
The History of the Old Testament

1. THE CREATION OF THE WORLD.—At one time dear children, the world in which we live did not exist. There was no land nor sea nor bright blue sky. There were no trees nor plants nor flowers. There was no person nor thing but God. He always was and always will be.

Then God made the world, the land, and the water; the sun, the moon, and the stars; the birds and the fishes and all the creatures of the earth.

Last of all, God made a man and a woman, whom He named Adam and Eve.

And God is so great and powerful that He made all these in six days, and out of nothing, by His word alone.

On the seventh day God rested from His work and blessed that day. For this reason the Jews kept it holy, and called it the Sabbath, which means to rest from labor. But after our blessed Lord was crucified by the wicked Jews the apostles chose Sunday, the first day of the week, as their day of rest, because on that day Our Saviour arose from the dead.

2. THE GARDEN OF PARADISE.—The home of Adam and Eve was a lovely garden, in which sweet-smelling flowers and ripe, juicy fruits grew. Pretty birds sang in the branches of the trees, and animals of every kind sported and played together. Everything was peaceful and beautiful.

God told Adam that he and Eve might eat of the fruit of every tree in the garden, except of one, and that one they must not touch.

3. THE FIRST SIN.—This was a very little thing to require; and, had our first parents obeyed God, they would have lived forever and would have been happy in this beautiful garden. But one day the devil tempted Eve to eat the forbidden fruit and told her that if she ate it she would become as great as God Himself.

Eve was foolish and wicked enough to believe this, and in spite of God's command she ate the forbidden fruit. Then, not satisfied with sinning herself, she coaxed Adam to eat of the fruit also, and in this way sin was brought upon the earth.

Almighty God was angry with Adam and Eve for disobeying Him. To punish them He drove them from the garden, and condemned them to spend the rest of their lives in labor and suffering, until they returned to the dust out of which they were made.

This terrible curse was to fall not only on them, but on all who came after them. But so great is the love of God for His creatures that, even in spite of their sin, He promised that He would send a Redeemer to save mankind.

4. CAIN AND ABEL.—Adam and Eve had many children. The first two were called Cain and Abel. Cain was a husbandman, or farmer, and Abel was a shepherd. They both offered gifts to God, and as Abel was a good man, his offerings pleased Our Lord; but those of Cain, who was wicked, did not please Him. At this Cain became angry and jealous of his brother, and at last hated him.

One day he asked Abel to go into the fields with him, and while they were there all alone the wicked Cain killed his brother. Then God cursed Cain for what he had done, and set a mark on him, and he went forth a wanderer on the face of the earth.

5. THE DELUGE.—Mankind was now divided into two classes: the good and the wicked. The first were the descendants of the pious Seth, a child given by God to Adam and Eve to console them for the death of Abel. The wicked were those who sprung from the murderer Cain. After a while the good and the bad married, and, as generally happens in such cases, in time all became wicked.

Then God commanded Noe, who alone remained holy, to build a large boat called an ark, and to go into it with his wife, his three sons and their wives, and take with him pairs of every kind of animal.

When this was done God sent a flood upon the earth. The rain poured from the heavens until the water had risen above the top of the highest mountain. Every living thing—men, women, and children, beasts, birds and reptiles—was drowned, except Noe and all that were with him in the Ark.

For a whole year the Ark floated safely on the waters, at the end of which time it rested on the mountains of Armenia.

Then Noe and his family, and every living thing that was with them, came forth. As soon as all were out, Noe built an altar and offered up sacrifice to God to thank Him for His goodness.

When you are older you will understand that the Ark was but a type of the Church of God, in which those who seek shelter are safe.

6. THE TOWER OF BABEL.—Noe and his three sons, whose names were Sem, Cham, and Japhet, began to cultivate the earth. After a while the number of people on the earth increased, and it was found that all could not live in the same place. Before separating they agreed to build a city with a tower that would reach to heaven, in which they would be safe in case of another deluge.

But God punished their pride by changing their language, so that they could not understand one another. Before this they all spoke the same language; now there were many languages. The city and tower were left unfinished, and the people scattered, going to different parts of the earth.

7. THE CALL OF ABRAHAM.—When Noe had lived nine hundred and fifty years, he died. About a hundred years after his death God ordered a holy man named Abram, who was afterwards called Abraham, to leave his own country and go into the land of Chanaan. And God promised Abraham that he should be the father of a great people, and that in him all nations should be blessed.

To try him, God at one time told Abraham to sacrifice his best beloved son, whose name was Isaac. Abraham hastened to obey, but just as he was about to kill his son, God sent an angel to stop him.

Abraham lived to the age of one hundred and seventy-five years, and was always the same pious man, ever ready to do the will of God. At his death his son Isaac succeeded him. Isaac had two sons, Esau and Jacob.

8. Joseph.—Jacob was the father of Joseph and of eleven other sons. Joseph was so good and so obedient that his father loved him better than any of his brothers. To show his love, Jacob gave Joseph a coat of many colors, which made his brothers very angry. One day they committed a wicked deed, and as Joseph told his father of it, they hated him all the more.

Some time after, Joseph was sent by his father to the field where his brothers were feeding their sheep. When he reached there they stripped him of his coat, threw him into a pit, and at last sold him to some merchants who passed by on their way to

Egypt.

Then the brothers dipped Joseph's coat in the blood of a kid, and sent it to their father. When the old man saw it he said: "It is my son's coat; a wild beast has eaten him;" and he wept for his beloved boy.

The merchants who bought Joseph took him to Egypt, where, by his piety and wisdom, he soon became a very great man and governor of the land.

9. THE FAMINE.—Nine years after Joseph had been sold there came a terrible famine, and Jacob sent ten of his sons to Egypt to buy corn. Benjamin, his youngest son, he kept at home, fearing that something would happen to him.

Now Joseph had charge of the corn in Egypt, and when his brothers came to him he knew them at once, though they did not know him. He pretended to take them for spies, and cast Simeon, one of the oldest, into prison. Then he bid the others go home to their father with the corn they had bought, promising to free Simeon if they would come back with their youngest brother, Benjamin.

The brothers felt that God was now punishing them for their wickedness, and went off quite sad. When they reached home they told everything to their father. At first Jacob refused to let Benjamin go, but when the corn was all eaten up he was obliged to consent.

10. THE CUP IN BENJAMIN'S SACK.—The brothers soon reached Egypt, and were at once taken to Joseph's palace. Joseph wept for joy when he saw Benjamin, and blessed the boy. He asked his brothers to dine with him, and waited on them himself. The next morning their sacks were filled with corn, and they started for home. They had not gone far when a servant came hurrying after them, to say that one of them had stolen a silver cup.

To prove that they had not done such a wicked thing, they went back; but when they were searched the missing cup was found, hidden in Benjamin's sack.

Now Joseph had ordered one of his servants to place the cup there, so as to try his brothers. When they saw it, they fell at Joseph's feet and offered to be his slaves; but he told them they might all go home, except Benjamin, who should be his slave.

At this, Juda, one of the brothers, begged Joseph to keep him for a slave, and let Benjamin go, saying that their dear old father would die of grief if Benjamin did not return.

11. JOSEPH MAKES HIMSELF KNOWN TO HIS BROTHERS.—Joseph knew by this that his brothers were no longer the bad men they used to be. All strangers were ordered to leave the room, and when they were alone Joseph said: "I am Joseph, your brother. Be not afraid, for God sent me to Egypt that you might have food when you needed it."

Then he embraced Benjamin and his other

brothers, gave them handsome presents, and sent them home to their father.

As soon as Jacob heard that his beloved son was still alive he started for Egypt, taking with him his whole family. Joseph hastened to meet his father, and seeing him, fell on his neck, weeping.

"Now shall I die with joy," said Jacob, "because I have seen thy face." Almost these same words were used, seventeen hundred years afterward, by the holy Simeon, when he saw our divine Saviour presented as a babe in the Temple.

Joseph gave his father and his brothers land on which to feed their flocks, and they became a great nation.

Seventeen years after his arrival in Egypt Jacob died, but Joseph lived to be a hundred and ten years old, and saw his grandchildren before his death.

Joseph's life was, in many ways, a picture of the life of our Saviour. Joseph was hated by his brothers on account of his virtues; Jesus, too, was hated. Joseph was betrayed and sold; so was Jesus. Joseph triumphed in the end, and was made governor of Egypt; Jesus was victorious over death, and is King of heaven and of earth. Joseph saved his brothers from dying by famine; Jesus Christ died to save us from the death of sin.

12. MOSES IS BORN.—After the death of Joseph, the Hebrews, who were the descendants of Jacob, increased so very fast that the king of Egypt was afraid they would become too powerful. To prevent

this he ordered that they should do all the hard work in the country, and, as that might not be enough, he commanded that every baby boy should be drowned as soon as he was born.

About this time a Hebrew woman had a little boy, whom she loved dearly. She wished to save her baby, and so for three months she hid him. When she could hide him no longer she made a basket of rushes, which she daubed over with slime and pitch, so that the water could not enter, and, with her heart almost breaking, she put her baby in it, and laid it in the high grass along the river's side. The baby's sister, whose name was Mary, hid near by to watch.

Shortly after, the king's daughter came down to bathe, and, seeing the basket, sent her servant for it. The princess opened it and saw a pretty little boy, and her heart was filled with pity for his poor mother. She made up her mind to save the child and bring him up as her son. The babe's sister now ran up to her, and asked if she should find a nurse for him: being told to do so, she brought his mother. The babe was named Moses, which means saved from the water.

13. MOSES' FLIGHT.—When Moses was forty years old he set to work to help his countrymen, who were suffering many hardships. This displeased the king, who ordered Moses to be put to death; but he fled from Egypt to Madian, in Arabia, where he became a shepherd.

14. THE BURNING BUSH.—One day, while Moses was watching his sheep, God appeared to him in a burning bush. Moses was surprised to see that the bush did not burn up, and went nearer to look at it. God commanded him to stand still and to take off his shoes, as the place was holy. At the voice of God, Moses fell on his face.

Then God told him that he was chosen to free the Hebrews, and for this he must go before the king; but, as he was slow of speech, his brother Aaron should be spokesman.

15. THE PLAGUES OF EGYPT.—Moses and Aaron went to the Egyptian king and told him that God had ordered him to free the Hebrews. The king not only

refused to do this, but even gave the people harder work than before. Moses and Aaron went again to the king, who refused a second time to do as he was told. For not obeying, God sent ten plagues on him and his people.

At first the water of the rivers was changed to blood; then frogs covered the whole country; after that the dust of the earth turned into small insects which troubled both men and beasts; next came a plague of flies which filled all the houses; and then a disease which carried off the cattle. The sixth plague was boils on men and animals; the seventh, a hailstorm which destroyed the grain and fruits; and, last of all, a dreadful darkness for three long days.

Before sending the tenth and most terrible plague, God ordered each Hebrew family to sacrifice a lamb on the fourteenth day of the month, and to sprinkle the door-posts of each house with its blood; then to roast the lamb and eat its flesh with unleavened bread—all of which was done.

That night God's angel visited the houses that were not marked with the blood of the lamb, and there was great mourning among the Egyptians; for in every home, from that of the king down to the poorest man, the oldest child lay dead.

Then the king sent for Moses and Aaron and bid

them go out of Egypt as fast as they could, before any more of the Egyptians would die.

16. THE PASSAGE OF THE RED SEA.—Moses started at once with all his people, but they had not gone many days when the king was sorry that he let them go, and, taking his army, went in pursuit of them. When the Hebrews, who were on the shores of the Red Sea, saw the army coming, they thought themselves lost, as there seemed no way to escape. But Moses bid them fear not, and stretching forth his rod over the sea, as God commanded him, the waters divided, rising like a wall to the right and the left, leaving a dry passage through which the people crossed over to the other side.

The Egyptians followed, but when Moses again stretched his rod over the sea, the waters rolled back to their place, and the king with his whole army was drowned. This passage through the Red Sea is a figure of Holy Baptism, by which we are freed from the slavery of sin.

17. THE QUAILS, THE MANNA, AND THE WATER IN THE DESERT.—When the Hebrews had crossed the Red Sea they came into a desert, and soon their food was all gone. They could find nothing to eat, but God in His goodness sent a number of quails into their camp, and caused a fine bread, called manna, to fall from heaven. Later on, when they reached Mount Horeb and had no water, God ordered Moses to strike the rock with his rod, and water at once

poured forth in great quantity.

The manna which was sent down to feed the hungry Hebrews, or Israelites, as they were also called, was a figure of the Most Blessed Sacrament, in which our divine Lord gives Himself as food for our souls.

18. THE TEN COMMANDMENTS.—Three months after leaving Egypt, the Israelites came to Mount Sinai. Here God called Moses up to the mountain and bid him tell the people that, if they remained faithful to the Lord, He would continue to protect them, and would make them a chosen people. God also commanded the people to prepare themselves for two whole days, so as to be ready for the third

day. On the morning of the third day it began to thunder and to lighten; a thick cloud covered the mountain, and the top of Mount Sinai seemed to be on fire. Then came the sound of a trumpet, that grew louder and louder until the people trembled with fear.

When Moses had led the people to the foot of the mountain, God spoke thus:

I. I am the Lord thy God. Thou shalt not have strange gods before Me.

II. Thou shalt not take the name of the Lord thy God in vain.

III. Remember thou keep holy the Sabbath-day.

IV. Honor thy father and thy mother.

V. Thou shalt not kill.

VI. Thou shalt not commit adultery.

VII. Thou shalt not steal.

VIII. Thou shalt not bear false witness against thy neighbor.

IX. Thou shalt not covet thy neighbor's wife.

X. Thou shalt not covet thy neighbor's goods.

The Israelites, who were trembling with fear, promised to do all that God commanded. Afterward Moses went up to the mountain again, and stayed there forty days and forty nights conversing with God, who gave him two stone tablets, on which were written the Ten Commandments.

19. THE GOLDEN CALF.—While Moses was living on the mountain the people began to complain, and going to Aaron, asked him to make them gods like those of the Egyptians. Thinking to quiet them, he told them to bring him the golden earrings of their wives and daughters. To his great surprise they did: so, being afraid to put them off any longer, Aaron made a golden calf of the earrings, and gave it to the people to worship.

When Moses came down from the mountain and found the people adoring this idol—dancing about it and eating and drinking like pagans—he was so angry that he threw down the stone tables on which the Commandments were written, and they were broken in their fall. Taking the Golden Calf he cast it into the fire, and ordered all who continued in idolatry to be put to death. Moses then returned once more to the mountain, and begged God to pardon his people. The Lord heard this prayer, and Moses having made two stone tables like the first God wrote the Ten Commandments on them. When Moses came down from the mountain this time, his face shone so brightly that he was obliged to wear a veil, for the people dared not look upon him.

20. THE TWELVE SPIES.—The Israelites stayed a year at Mount Sinai; then they began their march to the Promised Land, and when they had reached its borders Moses sent twelve men to explore the country. After an absence of forty days they returned, bringing with them some of the fruits of the country. Amongst these was an enormous bunch of grapes, borne on the shoulders of two men, besides pomegranates and figs. The land, they said, was "flowing with milk and honey," but its people were giants.

At this the Israelites cried out against Moses and Aaron for bringing them out of Egypt. To punish them the Lord declared that they should wander for forty years in the desert, and that not one of them who was over twenty-one years of age should ever enter into the Promised Land.

21. THE SIN OF MOSES.—The last year that the Israelites were in the desert, they encamped at a place where there was no water. God told Moses to strike a rock with his rod. Moses hesitated for a moment; then struck the rock, and water at once gushed forth. For the doubt of God's power God said that Moses should never enter the Promised Land.

22. THE BRAZEN SERPENT.—Shortly after, the people again murmured, asking why Moses had

brought them to a wilderness, where there was neither food nor water. God heard their wicked complaints and sent serpents into their camp, whose bite killed a great many. Moses prayed that God would have mercy on the people, and the Lord ordered him to make a brazen serpent and to set it up. He did so, and all that looked upon it were healed.

This serpent was a figure of Our Saviour nailed to the cross; for as the Israelites who looked upon it were cured, so all who with faith look up to Christ are cured of the wounds of sin. Think of this every time you see a cross.

23. THE DEATH OF MOSES.—The time had now come for Moses to die; so he called his people together, reminded them of all that God had done for them, ordered them to keep the Commandments, and named Josue as his successor.

When he had finished speaking he went up to the top of Mount Nebo, from which the Lord showed him Chanaan, the Promised Land. Full of faith and thanks to God for all His favors, Moses died at the age of one hundred and twenty years.

24. THE ISRAELITES ENTER THE PROMISED LAND.—After the death of Moses, the Lord commanded Josue to lead the Israelites across the river Jordan into Chanaan. On the banks of the river the same miracle that had taken place at the passage of the Red Sea was repeated; for the water rolled

back, leaving a dry passage. When the Israelites had crossed over they encamped near Jericho, where they celebrated the feast of the Pasch. This feast was kept every year in memory of their release from Egypt. Jericho was a large city, surrounded by strong walls. God commanded the Israelites to march around this city for seven days. On the seventh day they sounded the trumpets of jubilee and carried with them the Ark of the Covenant—a box made of most precious wood, covered inside and out with gold, in which were kept the two tables of the Law. At the sound of these trumpets and the shouts of the people the walls fell in, and the Israelites entered and took the city. In time Josue conquered all the country; and thus, after long wandering, the Israelites arrived in the Promised Land.

25. THE INGRATITUDE OF THE ISRAELITES.—Although Almighty God had been so good to the Israelites, and had given them such a beautiful country, they soon forgot all they owed Him, and fell into idolatry. To punish them the Lord for a while allowed their enemies to overcome them and make them slaves.

26. SAMUEL.—When slavery had taught the Israelites sorrow for their sins, God sent holy men, called judges, to set them free and to rule them. The last of these judges was named Samuel. His parents were very pious people, who for a long while had no children. They prayed God to send them a son; and

just as He listened to the prayer of Elizabeth, eleven hundred years afterward, so He heard their prayer and gave them Samuel.

When the little boy was three years old his mother took him to Heli, the high-priest, and consecrated him to God. One night, when Samuel was sleeping in the Temple, the Lord called him. The boy thought it was Heli, and ran to him, but the priest said: "I did not call thee, my son; go back and sleep." The call was repeated three times, so Samuel knew it was the Lord, and cried out: "Speak, Lord, for Thy servant heareth." Then the Lord told him that He was obliged to punish Heli and his two sons: the father because he was too easy with his sons, and had not punished them for their wickedness, and the sons because they offended Him by many sins. Some time after, the sons were killed in battle, and when Heli heard the sad news he fell backward and broke his neck.

Samuel succeeded Heli as judge, and ruled wisely and well; but when he grew old, he appointed his sons judges over Israel. The sons were not like their father: they did not fear God, and the people became dissatisfied and asked for a king. This did not please Samuel, because he wished that God alone should be King of Israel. But the Lord bid him do as the people wanted; so he anointed, as their king, Saul, a beautiful and brave youth of the tribe of Benjamin. At first God was with Saul and gave him the victory over his enemies; but he afterwards disobeyed God, and was cut off from the throne of Israel.

27. DAVID.—At the command of God, Samuel went to Bethlehem, to the house of Isai, whose youngest son, David, was chosen by God to replace Saul. David was in the fields, tending his father's flocks when Samuel arrived. Samuel sent for him and anointed him.

As the Spirit of the Lord departed from Saul he became sad; then he ordered his servants to find some one who could play upon the harp and cheer him with its music. One of the servants told him of David, who was a skilful player; so Saul sent for him, and was so much pleased with David's playing that he made him his armor-bearer.

28. DAVID AND GOLIATH.—A war broke out between the Israelites and the Philistines, their chief

enemy, and as the three oldest sons of Isai were in the army with Saul, David returned home to his father. When the two armies were drawn up opposite to each other, a terrible giant, named Goliath, came forth from the Philistine camp and dared any of the Israelites to fight him hand to hand. Although Saul was a great warrior, he and his entire army were frightened at this, and none of them dared meet Goliath. For forty days the giant repeated his challenge. At the end of that time David came to the camp to see his brothers. He saw Goliath, heard his words, and was grieved that no one had the courage to fight him. Going to Saul, David said: "I will fight this Philistine."

At first the king would not let him attempt it, but, as David insisted, the king gave him a suit of armor and a helmet of brass. David was not used to such things, and he could not wear them; but, choosing five smooth stones out of the brook, and taking his sling in His hand, he went forth to meet the giant.

Goliath seeing this fair young man come out to fight him, thought that he would have an easy victory, but when they came near to each other David took one of the stones that he carried with him, put it into his sling, and swung it rapidly round and round. The stone flew out and struck the giant on the forehead with such force that he fell to the ground. David ran up, drew the sword of Goliath from its sheath and cut off his head.

When the Philistines saw this they were frightened and fled, and the Israelites following killed many of them.

This victory of David over Goliath was a figure of Our Saviour's victory over the devil; for, as David conquered Goliath with a staff and five smooth stones, so did our blessed Lord conquer the devil by His cross and His five wounds.

After Saul's death David was chosen king of Israel. He ruled for forty years, and when he died he left a great kingdom and a great name.

29. SOLOMON.—David was succeeded by his son Solomon, who at first loved the Lord and walked in his father's footsteps. One night the Lord appeared to him, and bid him ask whatever he wanted. Solomon asked for wisdom to rule over his people with justice. The Lord was so well pleased with this that He gave him not only wisdom, but also riches, honor, and a long life.

One day two women came to the king, asking him to decide a dispute they had. The one said: "I and this woman lived together in the same house, and we each had a baby boy. One night her child died, and while I was asleep she took my boy and placed her dead child beside me in the bed. In the morning I saw that the child was not mine." The other woman denied this, and there seemed no way to settle the dispute. Then Solomon ordered the living child to be cut in two, and half to be given to one woman and half to the other. The true mother's heart could not bear that harm should come to her darling boy, and she cried out: "My lord, give her the child, and do not kill it!" But the other woman said: "Let it be divided." Then Solomon, pointing to the true mother, answered: "Give the child to this woman, for she is its mother." And the people were astonished at the wisdom of the king.

Solomon built a temple to Almighty God at Jerusalem. It was the grandest and most beautiful the world has ever seen. For twenty years Solomon did all that he could do for the glory of God, but when he grew old he fell into sin and oppressed his people until they became discontented and rebellious.

30. THE DIVISION OF THE KINGDOM.—At Solomon's death the Jewish people divided into two kingdoms, Israel and Juda. Jerusalem remained the capital of Juda, while Samaria became the capital of Israel. The people of Israel soon fell into idolatry, and although God did much to save them, both by humbling and by cheering them, they were so self-willed and stubborn that they would not obey His laws. At last, to punish them for their sins, He allowed the Assyrians, a pagan nation, to conquer them and make them slaves, and in a short time there was nothing left of them as a nation.

The people of Juda, too, gave themselves up for a while to idolatry and sin. To punish them, God allowed the Babylonians to burn the Temple of Solomon, destroy Jerusalem, and later on to carry the entire people of Juda to Babylon, where they were kept as prisoners for seventy years. At the end of that time, when they were truly sorry for their sins, God led the Jews back to their own country. They at once rebuilt Jerusalem and the Temple, and for two hundred years lived peacefully and happily.

About three hundred and twenty-three years before the birth of Our Saviour the Jews fought not only with other nations but among themselves, until at last the Romans, then the greatest nation on the earth, were called upon to settle their disputes. Soon the Romans with their armies filled the country, seized the government, and made Herod king of the Jews.

Thus ended the kingdom of Juda. The time had now come for Our Lord Jesus Christ to be born into the world to save man from sin, and open the gates of heaven, which had been closed by the fall of our first parents.

PART II
The History of the New Testament

1. ELIZABETH AND MARY.—Long, long ago there lived two holy women named Elizabeth and Mary, who were cousins. Elizabeth was an old woman, and as she had no little children, she and her husband, who was named Zachary, used to pray to God to give them a child. One day, when Zachary was at God's altar in the Temple of the Lord, the Angel Gabriel came to him and said: "God has heard your prayer. He will send you a child, whom you must call John; he will do much good to his people, and teach them about the Christ to come. He must never taste wine, because God will make him strong." Zachary was frightened when he heard all this, and said to the angel: "I am an old man and my wife is old," and he doubted what God had said to him by the angel.

2. ZACHARY IS PUNISHED.—Now God was angry with Zachary for doubting that He could send him a child, but not very angry, because Zachary was a good man; so God told the angel to tell Zachary that He was displeased with him, and would make him dumb until the baby John was born. So then and there in the Temple Zachary was made dumb. When he came out he could not speak to his friends, but made signs to them, so they knew he was dumb, and they said: "Something has happened: he has seen some sight—a vision."

3. THE ANNUNCIATION.—After six months had passed away, God sent this same Angel Gabriel to a town called Nazareth, where the Virgin Mary lived with Joseph, her husband. The angel went to Mary's house, and when he came into the room he said to her: "Hail, full of grace, the Lord is with thee; blessed art thou among women!" And Mary felt troubled, for she thought, "This is a strange way of speaking to me." Then the angel said to her, "Fear not, Mary, for thou hast found grace with God. Behold thou shalt conceive in thy womb, and bring forth a Son; and thou shalt call his name Jesus, He shall be great, and shall be called the Son of the Most High." And Mary said: "How can this be done?" And the angel said: "The power of God will do it." He told her of her cousin Elizabeth, who, old as she was, would have a son in three months. Then

Mary said: "Behold the handmaid of the Lord; be it done to me according to thy word." And the angel went away.

4. MARY VISITS ELIZABETH.—Mary was glad to hear about Elizabeth, and she went in haste to pay her a visit. Elizabeth was very glad to see her cousin, and thus saluted Mary: "Blessed art thou amongst women, and blessed is the fruit of thy womb; and why has God done this to me, that the mother of my Lord should come to me? You are blessed, Mary, because you believed; therefore God will do to you what He has said". Mary then sang a beautiful song the words of which God put into her heart: "My soul doth magnify the Lord, and my spirit hath rejoiced in

God my Saviour. Because He hath regarded the humility of His handmaid: for behold, from henceforth all generations shall call me blessed. Because He that is mighty hath done great things to me, and holy is His name." This is a part of the song which is called the "Magnificat." Mary stayed with Elizabeth for three months, and then she returned home.

5. JOHN IS BORN.—After a time Elizabeth's little boy was born, and all her friends came to see her and wish her joy. When the baby was eight days old they had a ceremony called the circumcision, and they said: "You must call him after his father's name;" but Elizabeth said: "No; call him John." And they were surprised, because none in her family were ever called by that name. As Zachary was dumb they made signs to him to know what name they should call the boy, and he showed them that he wanted something to write on. So they brought him a writing-tablet, and he wrote on it only these words: "John is his name." And they were surprised that he should know it. As soon as he had written this, God rewarded him for his obedience, and his tongue was loosed and he spoke, blessing God. The neighbors wondered, and told every one all about what great and strange things had been done. And Zachary was told by God many things his son John would do when he grew up to be a man.

6. THE BIRTH OF JESUS.—At this time there was a great king in Rome named Caesar, and he wanted to know how many people there were in the world; so he gave orders that every one should go to the town in which he was born to have his name written on a list. Joseph and Mary, you know, were living at Nazareth; but as that was not the town of Joseph's birth, he told Mary to get ready and come with him to the town of Bethlehem, because he was of the house and family of David. They went from Nazareth to Bethlehem; but when they got there every inn and every house in the town was full of people, and they had no place to sleep in. You may be sure Mary was tired; so Joseph, after looking about, found only a stable, to which he brought

Mary. Here Mary's little Son, Our Lord and Saviour Jesus Christ, was born. Mary was the best of mothers, and she did all she could for her Child. She wrapped Him up and put Him in the manger—probably because there was straw there, and it was warmer than any other place. The men who take care of sheep are called shepherds, and some of these men were minding their sheep that night when Jesus was born. All at once a lovely angel came to them when they were out in the fields, and all around the angel was a bright light from God—so bright that the shepherds were afraid. The angel said to them: "Fear not, I bring you good news and great joy, because this day is born to you a Saviour, Christ, in the city of Bethlehem. If you want to seek Him, I will tell you how; you will find the Infant wrapped in swaddling-clothes and laid in a manger." When the angel had said this a great number of angels came and stood with him, and they praised God, and in lovely voices sang a song: "Glory to God in the highest; and on earth peace to men of good-will." After the song the angels opened their wings and flew up into heaven. It must have been a grand, glad sight for these poor men to see! The shepherds thought so, and said to one another: "Let us go over to Bethlehem, and let us see this wonder that is come to pass, which the Lord has told us of by His angel." They left their sheep and went off in great haste to Bethlehem, and they there found Joseph and Mary, and the Babe lying in the manger. They knew then that the Child was the Saviour, and that what the angel had said was true; so they told every one what they had seen and heard. Mary kept all these things in her heart, and did not forget them. Then the shepherds went back to mind their sheep, and on their way they praised God.

7. THE THREE WISE MEN.—At this time there were three Wise Men who lived in the East, and they went to Jerusalem, to the king, whose name was Herod, and they said to him: "Where is He who is born King of the Jews? We have seen His star, and we have come to adore Him." Herod did not like to hear of any other king but himself. So he sent word to all the learned men in Jerusalem to come to him,

and he said to them: "Where should Christ be born?" And they answered: "In Bethlehem," because it was known long before that that was the town where Christ was to be born. Herod said to the three Wise Men in secret: "Go to Bethlehem and find out where the Child is, that I also may go and adore Him." They went, and found Jesus with Joseph and Mary, and they offered Jesus presents of gold and incense. The three Wise Men were tired, and they went to rest. In their sleep they had a dream, in which God told them not to go back to Herod: so they did not.

8. THE PROPHECY OF SIMEON.—When the Child was eight days old Mary and Joseph had that ceremony which I told you of before, and the Babe was circumcised and called Jesus. After forty days Joseph and Mary took Jesus to the city of Jerusalem, where the great Temple was, "to present Him to the Lord," and to offer a sacrifice, according as it is written in the law of the Lord, "a pair of turtle doves, or two young pigeons." Now, in Jerusalem there lived a very holy old man, whose name was Simeon, and he used to pray to God that he might not die until his eyes had seen the Saviour Jesus. So when

Joseph and Mary brought the Child Jesus into the Temple, a thought from God came into Simeon's mind, and he said to himself: "I will go to the Temple to-day." He went, and there he saw a man and woman with a Child, and he went to them and took the lovely Babe from Mary into his own arms. He knew he was right, and he said: "Now, Lord, I am ready to die because You have let me see the Saviour Jesus with my eyes." Mary and Joseph were surprised at all this, and Simeon saw surprise in their faces; so he blessed them, and he said to Mary: "This Child is set for the fall and the saving of many"—that is, many will believe in Him and so go to heaven, and many will not believe and so go to hell. Then he told Mary that she would have great sorrows—so great that they would pierce her soul like a sword.

9. The Flight into Egypt.—When Joseph went to sleep one night, an angel came to him and said: "Get up and take Mary and the Child into Egypt, and stay there until I tell you to return, for Herod has it in his mind to kill Jesus." Joseph called Mary and told her, and they set out at once for Egypt. When Herod found out that the Wise Men did not return, he was furious, because he knew they had seen the Child and would not tell him. He was a cruel, wicked man, and he told his soldiers to kill all the baby boys they could find under two years old. Just fancy how those mothers cried when the soldiers went up to them and took the babies from their arms, and out of their beds and killed them all! Herod hoped that the soldiers might find Jesus amongst them, and so kill Him! But they did not; and after a time Herod died, and Joseph returned with Jesus and Mary to Nazareth.

10. THE FEAST OF THE PASSOVER.—In those days there used to be a great feast in the Temple at Jerusalem every year, and people from all parts of the country used to go to Jerusalem for this feast.

Joseph and Mary used to go, too, every year. The Child Jesus was a lovely Boy, and was growing strong and tall and more lovely every year. When He was twelve years old Joseph and Mary took Him to Jerusalem for one of these feasts, and a great number of their friends and relations went too, and they all stayed there some days. On their way home again they missed Jesus. Mary thought He was with Joseph, and Joseph thought He was with Mary. When they found it was not so, they said: "Oh, He is with our relations;" but when they asked their friends they said: "No—we have not seen Him." So Mary and Joseph went back to Jerusalem and looked about for Him for three days. At last they went into the Temple, and there they found Jesus sitting down with a number of priests and learned people about Him, and He was asking them questions and answering theirs in a wise and clever way—so wise that all these learned men were surprised. When Mary saw Him, she said to Him: "Son, why hast Thou done so to us? Thy father and I have sought Thee with sorrow." Then Jesus answered and said to them: "How is it that you sought Me? Did you not know that I must be about My Father's work?" Mary and Joseph could not tell why He spoke thus to them, but Mary kept all these words in her heart to think over them. Then Jesus went back with them to Nazareth, and was subject to them—that is, He obeyed them in all things.

11. THE BAPTISM OF JESUS.—A good many years had now passed, and John, the son of Zachary, who had been living all this time in a lonely place—the desert—praying to God, was told by God that now he should tell the people what to do. So he left the desert, and came to the river Jordan, the same river that rolled back for the Jews hundreds of years before. Here John called all the people about, him, and told them of God: that they should never more be wicked. After he had baptized them he told them such holy things that at last the people said that he must be the Christ. But John was pained at this, and he told them that he was not worthy to tie the shoes of Christ—which meant that even as a servant he was not worthy to serve Jesus Christ.

One day Jesus also came to the river Jordan to be

baptized by John. When John saw Jesus coming, he said: "Behold the Lamb of God; behold Him who taketh away the sins of the world." After the baptism a wonderful thing took place. The sky opened, and the Holy Ghost, in the shape of a dove, flew down to Jesus, and a voice was heard by the people saying from heaven: "This is My Beloved Son, in whom I am well pleased." Jesus at this time was thirty years old.

12. THE MARRIAGE FEAST.—Jesus loved His Mother Mary very much, and He did what she asked Him to do. There was one day a wedding at a place called Cana, and Jesus and Mary were asked to it. At the feast all the wine was used, for there was not enough, and when Mary saw this she told Jesus that

there was no wine. Jesus did not want to use His power yet; but He could not deny His Mother, as we shall see. He said to Mary: "What is it to us if they have no wine?" But Mary knew in her heart that Jesus would do what she wanted. So she said to the servant-men who were waiting at the table: "What He tells you to do, do it." Now, in the room there were six large stone jars, with a little water in them, and Jesus, calling to Him the servants, said to them: "Fill the water-pots with water." And they filled them up to the brim. Then Jesus said: "Draw the water out now and take it to the butler;" and they did; but the man did not know, when he had tasted it, where the wine had come from, for Jesus had changed the water into wine. The guests at the table said: "Our host has kept the best wine for the last." This beginning of miracles Jesus did in Cana of Galilee, and manifested His glory, and His disciples believed in Him. Jesus then went to His own city, Nazareth.

13. THE DRAUGHT OF FISHES.—Such crowds of people used now to follow Jesus to hear Him speak of God that one day, when He was standing near the shore of a lake, they pressed so close to Him that He had to get away. He called two fishermen who were washing their nets, and He said to one of them, whose name was Simon: "Draw the boat back a little from the land;" and then, sitting in the boat, Jesus talked to the people on shore, and taught them many things. When He had finished speaking, Jesus did a very kind thing for the fisherman. He told the man to row out into the deep water, and let out his nets to catch fish. But Simon said to Him: "We have worked all night, Master, and have caught none; but, still, as You tell me, I will let down my net." And he did so; and the net was so full at once of fishes that it was not large enough to hold them. So Simon

called out to James and John his partners, and Peter and others, to come and help him; and they filled their boats so full with the fishes that they were almost sinking. Peter was surprised at this, and so were the others; and when they had brought their ships to land, they left them and stayed with Jesus. Jesus always chose poor men as His companions, and He gave them great honor. In this way, at different times, He called unto Him His disciples to help Him to teach and preach, and they were called Apostles of Jesus. There were twelve of them, and their names were: Peter, Andrew, James, John, Philip, Bartholomew, Matthew, Thomas, James, Simon, Jude, and Judas.

14. THE SERMON ON THE MOUNT.—Jesus was always doing good to the people, curing them when sick; and He had a kind way of telling them stories, to make them know what He meant.

One day Jesus went up a high mountain and He brought His disciples with Him, and a great number of people; and He gave them a sermon, and with His own lips taught them how to pray. He told them to "pray always," and then taught them that prayer you say so often—the "Our Father."

15. THE MAN CURED OF THE PALSY.—After that sermon on the hill, Jesus told the people that He had the power to forgive sin; and to show that He had this power He worked this miracle: He was one day

preaching to the learned men in a house in the town of Capharnaum, and the house was so full of people that no one could get in at the door. There was a poor sick man in the town who had the palsy so bad that he could not walk, so he asked four of his friends to carry him on his bed to the house where Jesus was. In the East the roofs are flat and have a hole in them, so that people can go on the roof for air. The crowd being great, they could not carry the sick man in by the door, but they carried him up on the roof and let him down on his bed through the hole to Jesus. Jesus was so pleased at their faith, and at their trying so hard to see Him, that when He saw the sick man He said: "Son, thy sins are forgiven thee: arise, take up thy bed, and walk." At once the man got up quite cured, and thanked Jesus, praising God. At this the people wondered, and said: "We never saw the like."

16. THE POOL OF BETHSAIDA.—After a time Jesus went to Jerusalem. Now at Jerusalem there was a pond of water called the Well of Bethsaida. God used to send, at certain times, an angel of His to this pond to stir it up. Many people, the sick and lame and blind, used to stay near this pond to watch for the angel; for when the angel visited the pond, the man who could get first into the water would be cured. There was one poor man who had been waiting at this pond for thirty-eight years, but he was so sick that when he used to try to get into the water after the angel had come, some other man, stronger

than he was, would get in first, and so be cured. Jesus heard of this sick man, and went to him, and said to him: "Wilt thou be made whole?" And the sick man said: "Sir, I have no man, when the water is troubled, to put me into the pond; for whilst I am coming, another goeth down before me." Jesus said to him: "Arise, take up thy bed and walk." And at once the man was made well, and he took up his bed and walked.

17. THE STORM AT SEA IN GALILEE.—One day Jesus said to His disciples: "Let us go over to the other side of the lake;" they had been teaching the people near a lake called Genesareth, and He got into a little ship with His disciples. After they had been out on the water a short time, Jesus, who was tired, went to sleep. When He was asleep a storm of wind came on, and the boat began to fill with water, and they were in danger. The disciples, being afraid, went to Jesus and awoke Him, and said: "Master, we perish." So Jesus, getting up, told the wind to be quiet, and the sea also, and it became quite calm.

18. THE DAUGHTER OF JAIRUS.—When the ship had crossed the lake and come to the shore, a man named Jairus came to Jesus and went down on his knees before Him saying: "My only little girl, just twelve years old, is dying;" and Jesus went with the man to his house; but such a crowd pressed around Jesus that they could not move easily. A sick woman touched the dress of Jesus, and was instantly cured. Just as they got near the house of Jairus, a servant came out and said to Jairus: "Do not trouble Jesus, for thy daughter is dead." Jesus hearing the servant say this, said to the girl's father: "Fear not; believe

only, and she shall be safe." When they went into the house—the father and mother and Jesus and a few others—they saw the little girl lying dead, and they were all in great sorrow, and wept bitterly. But Jesus said: "Weep not: the maid is not dead, but sleepeth." And the people laughed at Jesus in scorn, because they knew she was dead. But Jesus, taking her by the hand, cried out, saying: "Maid, arise." At once she came to life and got up, and Jesus told them to give her something to eat. The parents were very happy and surprised at this wonder that Our Lord did for them.

19. THE LOAVES AND FISHES.—Once a great crowd—five thousand people—followed Jesus to a lonely place, far away from a town, to hear Him preach. It was evening, and no one had anything to eat. So the disciples came to Jesus, and said to Him:

"Send away the people, that they may go to the towns and buy food." But Jesus said to them: "Give you them to eat." And they said: "We have no more than five loaves and two fishes, unless we go and buy food for all these people." Jesus said: "Make them sit down by fifties in a company." And they did so, and made them all sit down. And Jesus took the five loaves and the two fishes, and He looked up to heaven and blessed them; and He broke the bread and gave it to His disciples to give to the people. And all these five thousand people had so much to eat from the five loaves and the two fishes that, when they had had enough, twelve baskets were filled with the broken pieces. This was a great wonder, and it was done to show us what Jesus does on our altars.

20. JESUS WALKS ON THE SEA.—After this wonder Jesus told His disciples to go in a boat across the lake and wait for Him. Jesus liked to pray alone, so He sent away all the people and the disciples. The disciples waited for Jesus in the boat, and a storm came on with the night. Now Jesus saw the boat out in the lake, and He knew they were afraid, so He walked out on the sea—He did not swim, but walked on the water, just as we walk on land. When the disciples saw Jesus coming to them in this strange way they were afraid, and they said to one another: "It is a ghost." But Jesus spoke to them, saying: "Be of good heart: it is I, fear not." And Peter, who was in the boat, said: "Lord, if it be Thou, bid me come to Thee upon the waters;" and Jesus said: "Come." Peter, who saw how rough the sea was, and how the wind blew, was afraid, but he stepped out of the boat, and when he began to sink, he cried out, saying: "Lord, save me." And at once Jesus put out His hand and took hold of Peter's, saying: "Oh, thou of little faith, why didst thou doubt?" They walked together to the boat, and the wind ceased. The disciples, when they saw this, adored Jesus, and said: "Indeed Thou art the Son of God."

21. THE TRANSFIGURATION.—Jesus had now taught His disciples many things, and told them of many things that would happen to Him, and He made Peter the chief of His apostles. One day Jesus took Peter, James, and John with Him to a high mountain, and when He was there His face shone as the sun, and His clothes became white as snow, and two good men, Moses and Elias, who had lived long ago, were seen talking to Him. When the disciples saw this great sight they fell flat on their faces, and they heard a voice from heaven say: "This is My beloved Son, in whom I am well pleased: hear ye Him." Jesus saw how afraid His disciples were, and He went to them and touched them, saying: "Arise, and fear not;" and, lifting up their eyes, they saw no

one, only Jesus. After this Jesus told them that one of them would betray Him to His enemies, and that He would be put to death, but that after three days He would rise again.

22. JESUS THE CHILDREN'S FRIEND.—One day the disciples were talking to Jesus about heaven, and they wanted to know who would be the greatest in heaven. There was a little child passing at the time, and Jesus called the child to Him, and said to His disciples: "Amen I say to you, unless you be converted" (made good) "and become as little children, you shall not enter into the kingdom of heaven." Jesus then told them what a bad thing it was to teach sin to little children, or to one another; and said that it would be better for any one teaching sin to these little ones of His, that he had never been born, or that a stone should have been tied round his neck and that he should be drowned in the sea. You see Jesus loved little children who were good, and grown-up people must be good too, and as simple as little children. You must never tell anything wrong to another, or teach those younger than you sins, because you know now what Jesus says. Jesus at this time also told fathers and mothers how they should live, and husbands and wives. There were many mothers in the crowd, and they had their little children with them. When Jesus had done speaking, the mothers brought their little children to Jesus that He might lay His hands upon them and bless them; but the disciples thought it was too much trouble to

Jesus, so they told the mothers not to bring the children. But Jesus was not pleased at this, for He loved little children, and He said: "Suffer the little children, and forbid them not to come to Me for the kingdom of heaven is for such." And then Jesus blessed each little child. Little children ought to love Jesus very much for this.

23. THE BLIND MAN.—When Jesus and His apostles had come to a town called Jericho with a number of people, a blind man, who heard that Jesus was passing, called out to Him, saying: "Jesus, Son of David, have mercy on me!" And Jesus stood still, and told them to bring the blind man to Him; so the

people brought the blind man, and Jesus said to him: "What wilt thou that I should do to thee?" and the blind man said: "Master, that I may see." Then Jesus said to him: "Go thy way: thy faith hath made thee whole;" and at once he saw, and followed Jesus with the other people.

At times the people and apostles could not understand Jesus, and He would then explain what He meant by telling them stories.

24. THE GOOD SAMARITAN.—Once when Jesus was teaching, a man who was a lawyer thought he would tempt Jesus, so he said to Him: "Master, what must I do to possess eternal life?" And Jesus said: "What is written in the law?—how readest thou?" And the lawyer said: "It is written: Thou shalt love the Lord Thy God with thy whole heart, and with thy

whole soul, and with all thy strength, and with all thy mind: and thy neighbor as thyself." And Jesus said: "Thou hast answered right; this do, and thou shalt live." And the man said: "Who is my neighbor?" Jesus then told him this story: Once there was a man who was going a journey from Jerusalem to Jericho, and on his way some robbers met him. They tore off all his clothes, took his money, and struck him and hurt him, so that they left him like a dead man by the side of the road. After a time a priest went down the same way, and, seeing him, passed by. In like manner, a Levite, when he was near the place and saw him, passed by. But at last a Samaritan, being on his journey, came near him, and seeing him was moved with pity, and going up to him, bound up his wounds, pouring in oil and wine, and putting the man on his own mule, brought him to an inn, and took care of him. The next day he had to go away, but he left money with the owner of the inn, and told him to take care of the man, and that if the money was not enough he would give him more on his return. Then Jesus said to the lawyer: "Which of these three, in thy opinion, was neighbor to him that fell among the robbers?" And he answered: "He that showed mercy to him." Then Jesus said to him: "Go, and do thou in like manner." In this story Jesus teaches us who is our neighbor, and that we should do to others what we would like them to do to us. If you were hurt or sick you would like some one to be kind to you; you ought then to be always kind to others, to the ugly, dirty, and cross, as well as to nice people, because they are your neighbors. A neighbor in this sense does not mean only the person who lives next door, but every man, woman, and child.

25. WE MUST FORGIVE TO BE FORGIVEN.—One day Peter asked Jesus how often he should forgive his friends if they vexed or hurt him, would it be often enough if he forgave them seven times? But Jesus told him: No, that even if Peter were to forgive them, not seven times, but seventy-seven times, it was not enough; and then Jesus told him a story. Once there was a king who had a friend who owed him ten thousand talents, and the man had no way of paying this money. The king sent for him and said: "Pay me the money you owe me;" but the man said: "I cannot." Then the king ordered that all this man had and loved in the world should be sold in order that he should be paid. But the man fell on his knees and begged the king to wait and to have patience with him. The king had pity on him, and said: "Well, never mind; I forgive you, and I will not ask you to pay me the money at all." So the man thanked him and went away. Just as he went out of the house he met a friend of his who owed him one hundred pence, and he caught hold of him by the throat, and said to him in a rough way: "Pay me what you owe me!" His friend said: "Wait a little, and I will pay you." But he would not wait, but took him and put him in prison till he paid the debt. Some people who knew how kind the king had been to this man went and told the king how cruel he had been to his

friend. The king, hearing it, was very angry and sent for him. When he had come the king said to him: "You wicked man! I forgave you all your debt because you asked it, and you would not show the same mercy to your friend." So he was sent off to prison until he had paid all his debt.

Jesus told Peter this story to explain to him that we must forgive others if we wish the King (God) to forgive us. God forgives us very, very often, and yet you sometimes find it very hard "to make up friends," and to forgive and forget from your hearts when you have a little dispute.

26. THE LOST SHEEP.—Once when Jesus was teaching, a number of men who were sinners came about Him to hear Him, and there were present also some men who thought themselves very good. These

men complained because Jesus spoke to and ate with sinners; so Jesus told these men some stories. Once there was a man who owned sheep, and he was called a shepherd. He had a hundred sheep in a fold, and one day a little lamb got out of the fold and was lost. The shepherd left all the other sheep and went to look for this lamb. At last he found it, and the poor little lamb was tired; so he took it on his shoulders and carried it back to the fold. Then the shepherd, going home, told his friends he had found the lost lamb, and he said to them: "Rejoice with me, because I have found my sheep that was lost." Jesus told them what this story meant; that heaven was like the sheepfold—that the sheep were the people, and that the lost lamb was a wicked person—one who had once been good, but had become bad; the shepherd was God, who loved this wicked little lost lamb, and went after it to find it, leaving the good sheep behind. And Jesus further said that there was more joy in heaven at one sinner becoming good and doing penance than over ninety-nine good people who need not penance.

27. THE PRODIGAL SON.—Another story was, that once a man had two sons. He was a rich man, had a grand house, and lived in great state. But the youngest son thought the house and life too quiet: he wanted to go out into the world and enjoy himself, and have a good time. One day he came to his father and said: "I know you are going to divide some money between my elder brother and me; give me my share now, and let me go away." The father was pained at this; still he did not refuse his son, but gave him his share of money. After a few days this young son bid good-by to his father and brother, and took with him some bad companions, and left his father's house. He went away to a country a long way off, and there led a very bad, wicked life. In a short time he had spent all his money, and, you may be quite sure, his friends then left him, because he could treat them no more. What could he do then? He was in a strange country, and he had no money.

At last he was truly miserable—he was hungry and had no clothes. One day he went to a man and asked him for work; but he looked so poor and dirty that the man said: "I can give you no work in my house, but you may go to my farm and mind the pigs." So he went and minded the pigs, but he got no food except what the pigs did not like. This he found so hard, and he was so miserable, that he began to think of home and of the servants that his father had; and he said to himself: "How many servants in my father's house eat bread, and I am here dying of hunger;" so he said: "I will arise and will go to my father, and say to him: 'Father, I have sinned against Heaven and before thee; I am not worthy to be called thy son; make me as one of thy hired servants.'" He started at once on his journey to his father. The father loved his son, and used to look out every evening for him, hoping he would come back. One evening he was looking out as usual, and he saw, a "great way off," his son, and he went to meet him, and running up to him put his arms round his neck and kissed him. But the son fell on his knees and said to him: "Father, I have sinned against Heaven and before thee; I am not now worthy to be called thy son." But the father was so glad to see him that he kissed him again and again, and put fine clothes on him, and told his servants to make a great feast, because his son, who was lost and was as one dead, was found again. Then they had a great feast, and music and dancing. The elder son, who was out at work in a field, heard the music, and came to the house to see what it was for, asking one of the servants he met what it all meant. And the servant told him: "Your brother has returned, and your father has made a great feast because he has come back safe." At this the elder brother was very angry, and he would not go into the house. His father hearing it came out to him, and tried to coax him in; but he would not, and said to his father: "I have done all you asked me to do for so many years, and have been good, and have not spent your money, but you never made a feast for me like you have for my brother, who spent all his money and led a bad life." But the father said to him: "Son, thou art always with me, and all I have is thine; but it was fit that we should make merry and be glad, for this thy brother was dead and is come to life again; he was lost and is found."

This story, too, was told to teach us that God will forgive sinners; but we must be sorry like the young son was, and confess our sins to the priest, as he did to his father; and as he was willing to be a servant in his father's house because of his sins, so we must be humble and willing to suffer for our sins. The good son, you see, was doubly rewarded, for the father said: "Son, all I have is thine"—not only his own share, but his father's also.

28. THE RICH MAN AND LAZARUS.—Jesus told this story to His disciples: There lived once a very rich man, and he had a fine house and grounds. To the gates of this house a poor man, whose name was Lazarus, used daily to crawl. He was hungry and

covered with sores. He lay there at the gate in hopes the rich man would send him some crumbs to eat. But the rich man did not. He was dressed in grand clothes, and had rich food to eat, and plenty of wine to drink; but he never sent even a crumb to the poor man he knew to be at his gate. This poor man was very ill, and his sores were so bad that dogs used to come and lick them. At length Lazarus died, and the angels came and carried him to the place of rest where Abraham is. The rich man died also, "but he was buried in hell." When he was in hell and burning in pain and torment, he lifted his eyes and saw this poor man with Abraham. The rich man cried out: "Father Abraham, have mercy on me, and send Lazarus that he may dip the tip of his finger in water to cool my tongue, for I am burned in this flame." But Abraham said: "Son, thou didst receive good things in the world, food, and wine, and riches, and health, but Lazarus had not all these good things. He has now his reward and has comfort, and you have your reward in misery." Abraham told him besides that none could go from heaven to hell, or from hell to heaven.

Jesus had told His disciples many things, but there was yet a great deal for them to know. He had made Peter head of His disciples, because Peter had most faith and had said that Jesus was "the Son of the living God." He also told them that soon He would be put to a cruel death, and that one of His disciples would give Him up into the hands of His enemies—the Jews.

29. CHRIST RAISES LAZARUS TO LIFE.—In a village called Bethania lived another Lazarus, with his two sisters, Martha and Mary. Jesus loved this family very much, and often went to visit them. One day Martha and Mary sent word to Jesus that Lazarus His friend, was very ill. When the messenger told Our Lord, Jesus said: "Lazarus is sick only that the glory of God and My power may be shown in him." Jesus was staying then in the country; and two days after He had been told that Lazarus was so ill, He called His disciples and said to them: "Lazarus, our friend, is asleep, and we must go to Bethania and wake him up." But His disciples said: "Lord, if he sleep he shall do well." But Jesus meant that Lazarus was dead. So He said to them plainly: "Lazarus is dead, and I am glad for your sakes that I was not there, that you may believe: but

let us go to him." When they arrived at Bethania, Lazarus had been dead four days, and in his grave. In those countries people are buried the day they die. Martha, when she heard Jesus had come, went to see Him, and said to Him: "Lord, if Thou hadst been here, my brother had not died; but I know that if Thou askest God, He will give it Thee." Jesus asked where Mary was, and Martha said: "She is in the house with our friends and many Jews, who came to mourn with us; but I will go and tell Mary You ask for her."

When Mary heard that Jesus asked for her, she rose with haste, left her friends, and went to Jesus. Falling down at His feet, she said: "Lord, if Thou hadst been here, my brother had not died." Jesus, when He saw her tears, and the Jews who had followed her weeping also, was very, very sorry for her, and He was full of trouble. He asked: "Where have you laid (buried) him?" And they said to Him: "Lord, come and see." And Jesus wept. The Jews, therefore, said: "Behold, how He loved him!" But some of them said: "Could not He that opened the eyes of the man born blind have caused that this man should not die?" Jesus, when He came to the grave, over which there was a stone placed, directed them to "take away the stone." Martha, when she heard this, did not like to have it moved, and said to Jesus: "Lord, by this time he smells, for he is now buried four days." But Jesus told her to have faith, and she would see the power of God. So the stone was rolled away. Jesus then gave thanks to God, and cried out with a loud voice: "Lazarus, come forth!" At once, just as he was, all wrapped in cloths, out came Lazarus from his grave, and Jesus told them to untie the cloths. What joy it must have been to Martha and Mary, and how glad Jesus must have felt to see the joy of these friends! for Jesus likes to make people happy. This was, indeed, a great wonder, and all those who had seen it went about the country and to Jerusalem telling how Lazarus, who was four days dead, was brought to life again by Jesus. When the Jews and those wicked people who had power in Jerusalem heard of it, they were jealous of Jesus and hated Him. They made up their minds that the first chance they had they would kill Him.

30. Jesus rides into Jerusalem.—About a week after Lazarus had come to life again, Jesus took supper with Lazarus and Mary and Martha, and the next day He said to His disciples: "It is time we went to Jerusalem." When they had come to Mount Olivet, Jesus told two of His disciples to go to the next village, and that they would there find tied to a gate an ass with its young one, called a colt. No man had ridden yet on this colt. Jesus told them: "When you find this colt, the man you see minding it will ask you what you want, and you are to say you want the colt, for the Lord hath need of it, and then he will let you take it." And the disciples going, did as Jesus bid them. When they brought the colt to Jesus, it had no harness or saddle on, so they spread their clothes over its back, and made Jesus sit on it. A very great

crowd of people now came, and they cut down boughs of trees, carried palm-branches in their hands, and strewed their clothes and boughs along the way for Jesus to ride over. They shouted and sang, "Blessed is He that cometh in the name of the Lord!" and so they entered Jerusalem in great joy. The whole city came out to meet them, and they said: "Who is this?" and the people said: "This is Jesus." Jesus went to the Temple, and crowds came with Him, and they brought to Him the blind, and deaf, and lame, and dumb, and all sick persons, and Jesus cured them, so that they were all glad and filled with joy, even the little children calling out, "Hosanna to the Son of David; blessed be the Son of David!" The Jewish priests and learned men, hearing the children, were angry, and they asked Jesus if He heard what the children said. Jesus always loved little children, and must have liked their song best of all, for He said: "Yes, I hear. Out of the mouths of infants and of sucklings Thou hast perfected praise."

31. THE WIDOW'S MITE.—When Jesus was in the Temple, He saw a poor widow drop a farthing into the money-box, and Jesus was so pleased at her giving the little she had, that He called His disciples to Him and told them that this poor woman had given more than all the rich, and her reward would be greater, because she gave all she had, and the rich only gave what they did not want.

32. THE PASCHAL LAMB.—You remember that the Jews had some laws given them by God, which

they kept in great state. One was how to celebrate the great feast of the Pasch, when they killed a lamb and ate a strange kind of bread. When the time came Jesus told Peter and John to go to the city and prepare a room for this feast. Jesus told them that in the city they would meet a man, carrying a jug of water on his head, and that they were to follow this man into any house he entered; that they were to ask the owner of that house where was the room for Jesus and His disciples to eat the lamb, and he would show them a furnished room, all ready. In the evening Jesus came to this place with His twelve disciples, and sat down with them at the table, and ate what is called the Lord's Last Supper.

33. THE WASHING OF THE FEET.—After supper was over, Jesus got up from the table, and tied a

towel round Himself, and taking a basin of water, washed the feet of His disciples, and dried them with the towel. When Jesus came to Peter to wash his feet, Peter did not like to let Our Lord do such a humble act, and said: "Lord, dost Thou wash my feet?" and Jesus said, "Yes." But Peter said to Him: "Thou shalt never wash my feet." And Jesus answered him: "If I wash thee not, thou shalt have no part with Me." Rather than this should be the case, Peter said: "Lord, not only my feet, but also my hands and my head."

Jesus then told His disciples why He had washed their feet. He said: "You call Me Master and Lord: and you say well, for so I am. If then I, being your Lord and Master, have washed your feet, you also ought to wash one another's feet. For I have given you an example, that as I have done to you, so you do also." This was to teach His disciples, and us also, to be humble and clean (good) of heart. Jesus knew even while He was speaking that there was one of His disciples there who was not clean (good) of heart, and his name was Judas.

34. THE BLESSED SACRAMENT.—After Jesus had washed His disciples' feet, and whilst they were eating, He said: "Amen I say to you, that one of you is about to betray Me." The disciples were sorry to hear this, and each said: "Is it I, Lord?" And Judas, that did betray Him, said: "Is it I, Rabbi?" (Master.) He saith to him: "Thou hast said it." And whilst they were at supper, Jesus took bread, and blessed and broke, and gave to His disciples, and said: "Take ye and eat, this is My body." And taking the chalice, He gave thanks, and gave to them, saying: "Drink ye all of this, for this is My blood."

My dear children, this was the greatest, kindest, and most loving act that even God could do. Jesus could do no more than this. Never forget these words of Jesus: "This is My body," and "This is My blood." Jesus, then, at this feast, changed the bread into His body and the wine into His blood. No one can understand this, but when you are older you will know a little better. When you go to church, and bend your knee at the altar, you do so because you are told "the Blessed Sacrament" is there. You know now how it came there. The Blessed Sacrament is Jesus. Jesus gave us Himself at that Last Supper; and although we cannot see Him as He was then, as a man speaking to His disciples, yet the Blessed Sacrament is Jesus, and He is there on our altar, hidden in that "White Host," the very same good, kind, loving Jesus who was speaking to His disciples at the Last Supper. We ought to go often to our churches to see Jesus and talk to Him, to ask Him for everything we want; no little thing is too small and no big thing is too great to ask Jesus for, and you know He loves little children more than He loves grown people.

The Passion of Jesus

The sad time had now come when Jesus was to be so cruelly put to death, and for us. We must never forget that it was for each of us that Jesus died.

35. THE BETRAYAL OF JUDAS, AND PETER'S DENIAL.—Some days before, Judas, the bad disciple, had gone to the Jewish priests and offered to betray Jesus to them. For this they agreed to give thirty pieces of silver. While Our Lord and His disciples were at the Last Supper, Judas left the room, to carry out his wicked bargain. Jesus now was sad because He knew that the time had come for Him to suffer. Jesus told this to His disciples, and that soon He must leave them; but Peter said that he would never leave Jesus, but would die first. Jesus then said to him: "Before this very day is over, and before the crock crows, you will deny Me three times—you will deny that you know Me."

36. JESUS IN THE GARDEN.—Jesus now went to a garden called Gethsemani with His disciples. He was very sad, and He told them not to follow Him, but to stay where they were for a little, as He wished to pray alone. Jesus then went by Himself, and prayed, saying: "My Father, if it be possible, let this chalice pass from Me. Nevertheless, not as I will, but as Thou wilt." Jesus then went back to His

disciples, but He found them all asleep, and He said to Peter: "What! could you not watch one hour with Me? Watch ye and pray, that ye enter not into temptation; the spirit, indeed, is willing, but the flesh is weak." Three times Jesus went and prayed and used the same words, and each time found the disciples on His return fast asleep. Jesus was in such sorrow and trouble in these prayers that He was bathed in agony with sweat, which became as drops of blood trickling down to the ground. He saw all the sins of the world then, yours and mine, and He saw, too, that many, even after He had died for them, would not love Him, but would sin and grieve Him to the very end. He taught us in this agony of prayer how we ought to pray to God to be spared a trial, but at the same time to say, no matter how much it hurts us, "God's will be done." After these prayers Jesus went again to the disciples and awoke them, and said: "Rise; let us go; behold, he is at hand that will betray Me."

37. JUDAS BETRAYS JESUS.—When they had gone a little way, they met a great crowd of people and soldiers, and Judas was with them. Judas had told the soldiers that the man he would kiss would be Jesus, and to take that man. So Judas went up to Jesus, and said: "Hail, Master," and kissed Him; and Jesus said to him: "Judas, dost thou betray the Son of man with a kiss?" The soldiers then went to take Jesus, but Peter took out his sword and cut off the ear of one of them. Jesus told him to put away his sword, and touching the man's ear, He healed it, and gave Himself up quietly to the soldiers. When the disciples saw that Jesus was taken they ran away; Peter and John remained.

38. JESUS BEFORE THE HIGH PRIEST.—The crowd led Jesus to the house of a ruler named Annas, who asked Jesus many questions, and Jesus answered that He had not taught in secret; for saying this, one of Annas' servants gave Jesus a blow.

39. PETER DENIES JESUS.—When Jesus was in the house of Annas, Peter was outside in the courtyard of the house, where there was a fire burning, for it was cold; and about him were many people, soldiers and servants. While Peter stood at the fire very sad, a servant woman came to warm herself also, and said: "This man was with Him;" but Peter said: "Woman, I know Him not." After a little, a man said: "Thou also art one of them." But Peter said: "O man, I am not." And again, in an hour, another man

said: "Of a truth, this man was also with Him." Then Peter again, with many strong words, said: "Man, I know not what thou sayest." Just as he spoke the cock crew three times. Jesus was then passing through the court of Caiphas, another ruler, to whom Annas had sent Him, and He turned and looked at Peter. Peter then remembered what Jesus had said, that he would deny Him three times before the cock crew, and "Peter, going out, wept bitterly." The men that held Jesus struck Him cruel blows, jeering at Him, and crying out: "Say who it is that has struck You?" but Jesus remained silent.

40. CAIPHAS.—Jesus, when He was before Caiphas, was asked if He was "the Christ, the Son of the Blessed God?" and Jesus answered: "I am." Caiphas did not believe this, and said it was a wicked thing to say, and gave Jesus up into the hands of the people, to be taken the next day to the ruler, Pilate.

41. PILATE.—Jesus was brought by the people to Pilate, who asked what He had done; and when Jesus had answered, he said: "I find no fault in the man;" but the people only cried out all the more that Jesus was a disturber. Now, it was a feast-day, and it was the custom on those days, as an act of mercy, to release some man who was imprisoned for his crimes. So Pilate, who wished to make peace with the people, and perhaps get the release of Jesus, said

to them: "There is in prison a man named Barabbas, who did a murder; shall I release him to you, or shall I release Jesus?" The people said, "Let us have Barabbas, and crucify Jesus." But Pilate said to them: "Why, what evil hath He done?" But they cried out the more: "Crucify Him." So Pilate released Barabbas, and gave Jesus up to them.

42. THE SCOURGING.—Pilate thought that if he made Jesus suffer, the people's hearts would be touched and he could save Him: so he had Jesus scourged. You do not know what this word scourged means—it means whipped or flogged. But such a painful flogging!—you cannot imagine it!

43. THE CROWNING OF THORNS.—After that dreadful scourging, an old purple dress was put upon Jesus, a reed in His hand, and on His head a crown of thorns. They made Jesus a mock king. Coming up to Him, they mocked Him, and bending down before Him, said: "Hail, King of the Jews." Then they spat at Him, and struck Him, pressing the thorns deep into His head by their blows. How it must have hurt Jesus! How He suffered for those naughty thoughts we have sometimes! Often when you are asked why you have done a naughty thing, you will say, "I don't know; it came into my head." When these things come into your head, think for a moment of the crown of thorns on the head of Jesus, and you will not do wrong.

44. PILATE AND THE JEWS.—When Pilate saw what a dreadful state Jesus was in after all this cruel work, he thought that if he was to show Jesus to the people they would have pity; so he led Jesus out on a balcony, and said to the people:"Behold the Man!" But they had no pity, and cried out: "Crucify Him." Pilate saw it was of no use to try to save Jesus, but he was afraid to lose the favor of the people, and said to them: "He is a just man." Then he called for a basin, and washed his hands before the people, to show that his hands were clean of the death of Jesus. And he said to them: "I am innocent of the blood of this just man; look you to it." And the people cried out: "His blood be upon us, and upon our children." Pilate then said Jesus was to die, and gave Him up to the Jews.

45. THE WAY OF THE CROSS.—At that time it was the custom to crucify people who were ordered to be killed for great crimes. In our country we hang people, and in France they cut off their heads; but in the country where our Saviour lived they crucified, that is, nailed and tied a person to a cross until he died.

Jesus, then, all weak and torn and bleeding, was led out of Pilate's house by the people, and they made Him carry on His shoulders the cross on which He was to die. What a sad sight it must have been for Mary, His mother, and His disciples and friends to see! Even the women and children of the Jews cried for very pity when they saw Jesus bending under the weight of the great cross He was carrying. Jesus turned to these poor women and said: "Daughters of Jerusalem, weep not over Me: but weep for yourselves and for your children." The place to which Jesus had to carry His cross was called Calvary. It was where all the bad Jews were put to death. With Jesus were two wicked men who were also going to Calvary to be put to death. Jesus was so weak when He was carrying His cross that He fell down three times. At last He could carry it no further, and the soldiers made a man named Simon, who was passing by, carry the cross the rest of the way.

46. JESUS IS NAILED TO THE CROSS.—When they arrived at Calvary, the cross was put on the ground, and the soldiers took Jesus and stripped off His clothes. Then Jesus was laid upon the cross, and men came with a hammer and three nails. They roughly pulled our Saviour's hand to one side of the cross, and drove the large nail through it, fastening it to the cross; they did the same with the other hand. The feet were crossed over each other, and the one nail driven through both, and so Jesus was fastened to the cross. The nails were large, to bear the weight. What pain it must have been! Fancy each blow of the hammer driving the nail through the flesh! How sick Mary must have felt at the dreadful sound of the hammer! We cannot even imagine the pain of Jesus. We would scream and cry out if a pin was put through our hand; but Jesus was quite silent.

47. ON THE CROSS.—Have you seen men put a large stone, or pillar, or pole into the ground? They first dig a deep hole; then they tie ropes to the pole, and place one end of the pole just by the hole. Then they go a good many feet off and pull on these ropes. The pole slowly rises up, and goes into the hole with a sudden jerk. That is how the cross on which Jesus was nailed was jerked into the hole. That jerk must have been a terrible agony. The wounds in the hands and feet must have been torn larger by it, and must have bled more. At the foot of the cross stood Mary and John. You remember that Simeon had told Mary, long ago that a sword of sorrow would pierce her heart; and what sorrow could be greater than to see a good, tender Son suffer such pain at the hands of cruel men? When

Jesus was hanging there in this cruel state, the Jews mocked Him, saying: "He saved others: let Him save Himself if He be Christ." And the soldiers also mocked Him, saying: "If Thou be the King of the Jews, save Thyself;" and they wrote on the top of His cross, in scorn, these words in Latin: IESUS NAZARENUS, REX IUDÆORUM, that is, "Jesus of Nazareth, the King of the Jews." That is what the "I.N.R.I." means on the crucifixes you see, "Jesus of Nazareth, King of the Jews." But Jesus still loved and prayed for the wicked Jews, saying: "Father, forgive them, for they know not what they do."

48. THE THIEVES.—The two bad men, who were thieves, or robbers, were also crucified with Jesus, being put at each side of Him. One of these robbers mocked Jesus too, saying: "If Thou be Christ, save Thyself and us." But the other robber said to him in rebuke: "We suffer justly, for we receive the due reward of our deeds; but this man hath done no evil." And he said to Jesus: "Lord, remember me when You go to heaven." And Jesus said to him: "Amen I say to thee, this day thou shalt be with Me in paradise" (heaven).

49. JESUS SPEAKS TO MARY.—When Jesus saw Mary standing with John at the foot of His cross, He said to Mary: "Woman, behold thy son," and to John: "Behold thy Mother." And from that hour the disciple took her as his own Mother. Jesus, in saying this, gave Mary to us all as our Mother.

50. JESUS DIES.—Jesus had now been hanging in torture on the cross for three hours. He was in such pain of body and soul, that He called out: "My God, my God, why hast Thou forsaken Me?" He then said: "I thirst." A soldier who was near dipped a sponge in vinegar, and putting it on a spear, lifted it up to Jesus, who, when He had moistened His lips, cried out with a loud voice: "It is consummated," and then with a great cry of prayer: "Father, into Thy hands I commend My spirit," He bowed His head and died. The soldiers were filled with fear, and cried out: "Indeed, this was the Son of God"—for the earth trembled, the rocks split, the sun was darkened, the graves opened, and the dead arose. The people went back to Jerusalem full of fear. Later a soldier opened the side of Jesus with a spear, and blood and water came out of the wound.

51. JESUS IS PUT IN THE TOMB.—Joseph, a rich man, and a ruler, who believed in secret in Jesus, went at night to Pilate, and asked leave to take the body of Jesus and bury it. Pilate gave leave. So Joseph and his friends took down the body of Jesus from the cross, and wrapped it in white cloths and sweet spices, and put it in the tomb. The tomb was a new one, and cut in a rock, and had a great stone to close it up. Joseph had intended it for his own body when he died. The rulers knew that Jesus had said He would rise again from the dead in three days, so they sent a guard of soldiers to watch the tomb, for they said the disciples will steal away the body and

say He has risen, and so people will believe. So Pilate put his great seal on the tomb.

52. THE RESURRECTION.—The third day had now come. It was the early morning, and the soldiers were at watch, when all at once the earth shook, and an angel came to the tomb and rolled back the stone, and Jesus came out and showed Himself to the soldiers, all glorious and beautiful. His face shone like the sun, and the soldiers, afraid, ran away and told the rulers. The rulers, who were now afraid that the Jews would believe, gave the soldiers a great sum of money, and told them to tell the Jews that the disciples had stolen the body. This the Jews believed. Mary Magdalen and other women came that same morning to the tomb with spices. On their way they asked one another how they should roll

away the large stone from the door of the tomb, to put in their spices. But when they arrived they found the stone removed, and the body of Jesus gone. Mary Magdalen left at once to tell the apostles that the body of Jesus was gone. The other women looked into the tomb, for they saw a bright light, and there sat an angel, who said to them: "Be not afraid: you seek Jesus of Nazareth, who was crucified: He is risen; He is not here; behold the place where they laid Him. But go tell His disciples and Peter, that He goeth before you into Galilee, there you shall see Him, as He told you." But the women ran away in a fright, and told no one.

53. JESUS APPEARS TO MARY MAGDALEN.—Mary Magdalen ran and told Peter and the other disciple whom Jesus loved. "They have taken away the Lord out of the sepulchre, and

we know not where they have laid Him." Peter and John ran, too, to the tomb, but they could find nobody, and returned to their homes. Mary stayed at the tomb weeping, and stooping down and looking into the tomb, she saw two angels in white, and they said to her: "Woman, why weepest thou?" She said to them: "Because they have taken away my Lord, and I know not where they have laid Him." When she turned round she saw a man standing, whom she thought was the gardener, and she said to Him: "Sir, if thou hast taken Him hence, tell me where thou hast laid Him, and I will take Him away." Jesus (for it was Jesus) said to her: "Mary." She, turning, said to Him: "Rabboni" (Master). Jesus then told her to go and tell His apostles, and say to them: "I ascend to My Father and to your Father, to My God and your God;" and Mary did as she was told.

54. JESUS APPEARS TO HIS APOSTLES.—The apostles were that day in a room, with the door closed, afraid of the Jews, when Jesus came in, they knew not how, and said to them: "Peace be to you;" and when He had said this, He showed them His hands and His side; and they were glad to see Him. Thomas, who was one of the disciples, was not present when Jesus was there, and on his return the other disciples said to him: "We have seen the Lord." But he said to them: "Except I shall see in His hands the print of the nails, and put my finger into the place of the nails, and put my hand into His side, I will not believe." When eight days were

passed, the disciples were again in the same room, and Thomas was with them. Jesus came, the doors being shut, and stood in the midst, and said: "Peace be to you." Then He said to Thomas: "Put in thy finger hither, and see My hands; and bring hither thy hand and put it into My side; and be not faithless, but believing." Thomas answered, and said to Him: "My Lord and my God." Jesus said to him: "Because thou hast seen Me, Thomas, thou hast believed; blessed are they that have not seen and have believed."

55. PETER.—Jesus came another time to His disciples, and this time He asked Peter three times if he loved Him. And Peter each time said to Him: "Yes, Lord, Thou knowest that I love Thee;" and each time he said it Jesus told him, "Feed My

lambs," and the last time, "Feed My sheep." In these words Jesus meant to show that Peter was the chief of the apostles; the lambs were meant to show the children of the Church, and the sheep are the priests. Since then the Church has always had one to succeed Peter, who is called the Pope. We are the children (the lambs), and the priests (the sheep) teach us. But the Pope (Peter) guides us all—lambs and sheep, people and priests.

56. THE PROMISE OF THE HOLY GHOST.—Jesus had often shown Himself to His disciples, and on one occasion when He came to them He breathed on them, and said to them: "Receive ye the Holy Ghost; whose sins you shall forgive they are forgiven them, and whose sins you shall retain they are retained." Jesus in saying this gave power to His apostles and to His priests to forgive our sins if we confess them and are sorry for them. He taught them many things they had not known before. Forty days after Jesus had left the tomb and risen from the dead He came again to the disciples, and told them to stay in Jerusalem for some days, for He was about to leave them, but would send the Holy Ghost to comfort them.

57. THE ASCENSION.—After this Jesus went with His apostles to Mount Olivet. There He blessed them, and as He was blessing them the wonder and power of God were shown. Slowly, and in a bright light, Jesus was lifted from the ground and was raised up into the skies—into heaven—as they strained their eyes to look after Him. They were sorry to see Jesus go from them, and they remained in awe and wonder, looking up where Jesus had gone. At last two angels in white garments spoke to the apostles, and told them: "This Jesus, whom you have seen ascending into heaven, shall come again." The apostles praised God, and went back into Jerusalem, as Our Lord had commanded, to wait for the Holy Ghost.

You have now read, dear children, most of the stories of the Old and New Testament. Read them often, and when you are older you will never forget that these stories were told for your good, and in the hope that the seed sown in childhood's years may produce fruit even to the end of your days.

The Feasts and Fasts of the Year

The Feasts of the Church are certain days on which the Church celebrates the memory of particular mysteries of our holy religion or the glory of the saints.

Some of these are holy-days of obligation, on which, as on Sunday, we must hear Mass and do no servile work.

That these holy-days and feasts may not be forgotten, the Church divides the year into three parts namely: (1) from Advent to Lent; (2) from Lent to Pentecost; (3) from Pentecost to Advent again.

ADVENT, which means coming, is the time between three and four weeks before Christmas. During this time we must by penance, fasting, and prayer prepare for the celebration of the first coming upon earth, or the birth, of Our Lord. During Advent the priest wears purple vestments.

CHRISTMAS is the most beautiful of all the feasts of the year. It is particularly the feast of children, because on that day Our Saviour Jesus Christ was born—a child to the world.

On Christmas-day every priest is permitted to say three Masses. These Masses are supposed to figure the three births of Our Lord, namely, of His Father from all eternity, of the Blessed Virgin at Bethlehem and in the souls of men by grace.

The day after Christmas is the feast of St. Stephen. He was the first martyr, and was stoned to death by the Jews.

Then follow, January the first, the CIRCUMCISION, which reminds us that on the eighth day after His birth Our Saviour first shed His blood, and, a few days later, the EPIPHANY, telling us of the visit of the three kings or Wise Men who came from the far-off East to adore the babe Jesus.

On the second of February is the feast of the PRESENTATION OF OUR SAVIOUR IN THE TEMPLE. This feast is also known as CANDLEMAS, because on that day the Church blesses the candles to be used for religious purposes during the year. The candles which are blessed may be used by the faithful either at their private devotions or when the sick are to receive the sacraments.

Lent begins with ASH WEDNESDAY, which is so called because on that day ashes are blessed and put on the heads of the people to remind them that they are made of dust, and will one day become dust again, in the grave.

During the forty days of Lent the *"Gloria in Excelsis Deo"* is not sung at Mass, and the priest again wears purple vestments. All amusements are put aside, and, in imitation of Our Saviour's fast of forty days in the desert, the faithful are commanded to fast and do penance for their sins.

On PASSION SUNDAY, which is the second Sunday before Easter, the crucifix and pictures in the church are covered, to remind us of the sorrow and sufferings of Our Lord, and remain so till Holy Saturday.

On PALM SUNDAY, which begins Holy Week, palms are blessed and given to the people, and are carried in procession around the church, to call to mind the entry of Christ into Jerusalem, when the people spread palms before Him, and sang praises in His honor.

On HOLY THURSDAY, the institution of the Blessed Sacrament at the Last Supper is commemorated. On this day the Sacred Host, which is to be consumed by the priest at the Divine Office of the next day, is kept on a side altar, called the *Repository*, decorated with flowers and lights. This *Repository* is visited by the people, who pray there and adore our blessed Lord in the Sacrament of His love. From the Mass of Holy Thursday to the Mass of Holy Saturday no church bells are rung, in order to show the great sorrow of the Church.

On GOOD FRIDAY, the day on which Our Saviour died on the cross for us, the Church does all she can to make us feel how solemn is the event she celebrates. The altar is bare, for the Blessed Sacrament is not there, and the priest has on black vestments during the mournful ceremonies which conclude with the Adoration of the Cross.

HOLY SATURDAY, the day on which Our Lord's body lay in the tomb, is passed in silence and meditation. On this day at Mass is blessed the new fire, struck from a rock, an image of Christ, who is both a light to the world and a rock to His Church. Then the blessing of the Paschal candle follows. After this the twelve prophecies that foretold the coming of Our Saviour are read, and then the water to be used in Baptism is blessed.

EASTER SUNDAY is a feast in honor of Our Lord's rising from the dead on the third day after His crucifixion, and is one of great joy in the Church.

The first Sunday after Easter is called LOW SUNDAY; on that day in the early times of the Church newly-baptized persons wore for the last time the white robes that were put on them at their baptism.

The Monday, Tuesday, and Wednesday before Ascension Day are called ROGATION-DAYS, or days of prayer, when the Church wishes her children to pray for all things necessary for their spiritual and worldly good.

ASCENSION DAY is the fortieth day after Easter. This feast is kept in memory of Our Lord's ascension into heaven from the top of Mount Olivet in presence of His blessed Mother and His apostles and disciples.

Ten days after the Ascension is the feast of PENTECOST or WHIT-SUNDAY, kept in honor of the coming of the Holy Ghost upon the heads of the apostles in the form of fiery tongues.

TRINITY SUNDAY is the Sunday following Pentecost. On this day the Church honors in an especial manner the mystery of the Most Blessed Trinity—three divine persons in one God: the Father, the Son, and the Holy Ghost.

Thursday in the first week after Trinity Sunday is the great feast of CORPUS CHRISTI, when the Church honors the body and blood of Our Lord really present in the Most Holy Sacrament of the Eucharist.

Besides these feasts in honor of Our Lord, there are others that remind us of His Mother. One of these is the ANNUNCIATION, which is kept on the 25th of March in memory of the Angel Gabriel being sent to our blessed Lady to announce to her that she was chosen of all women to be the mother of the world's Redeemer. Another is the Assumption, in memory of the Blessed Virgin being taken up, at her death, body and soul into heaven.

There are other feasts, such as those of Sts. Peter and Paul, St. John and other apostles, together with the Martyrs and Confessors. All these end and are included in the great feast of ALL SAINTS when the Church honors all the known and unknown saints, so that none may be forgotten.

On ALL SOULS' DAY, which closes the Church year, we pray for the poor souls in purgatory, that they may be freed from their sins and soon see the joys of heaven.

Besides these feasts, all Catholics must keep certain fast-days. Among these are the Ember-days, which occur four times a year, namely, on the Wednesdays, Fridays, and Saturdays, which follow December 13th, the first Sunday of Lent, Pentecost, and September 14th. The object of the fast is that we may purify our souls and do penance as we begin each quarter of the year.

It is not enough for us to know these feasts and fasts, but we must keep them as the Church commands; for when we obey her we obey the voice of God, and may then hope to share with Him the never-ending joys of heaven.

www.ingramcontent.com/pod-product-compliance
Lightning Source LLC
Chambersburg PA
CBHW081347070526
44578CB00005B/753